Once upon a time
Santa Claus,
Cupid and
the Easter Bunny were
on vacation enjoying a picnic
and sharing stories of their
holiday adventures.

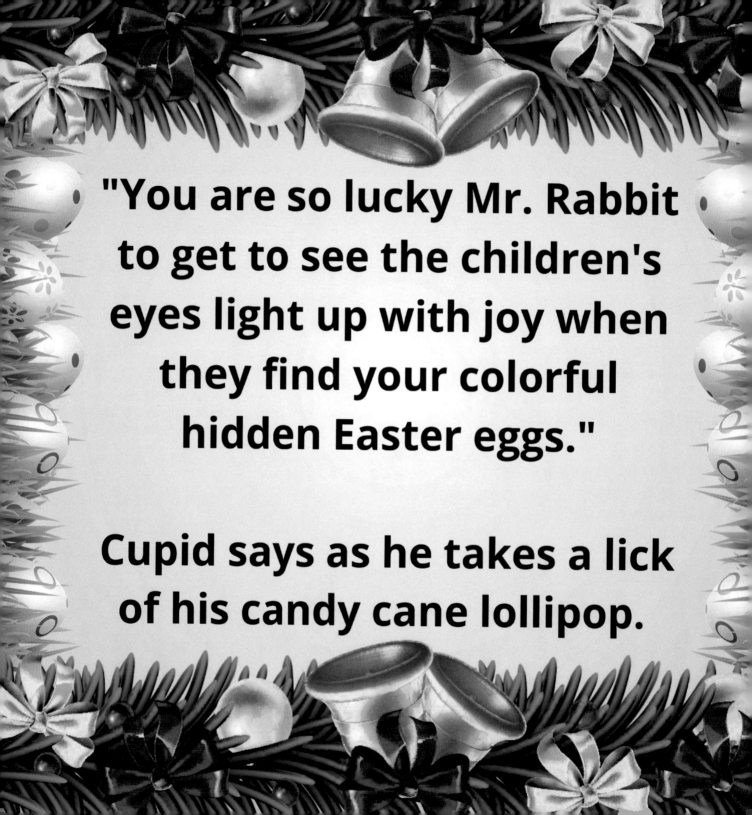

"You are so lucky Mr. Rabbit to get to see the children's eyes light up with joy when they find your colorful hidden Easter eggs."

Cupid says as he takes a lick of his candy cane lollipop.

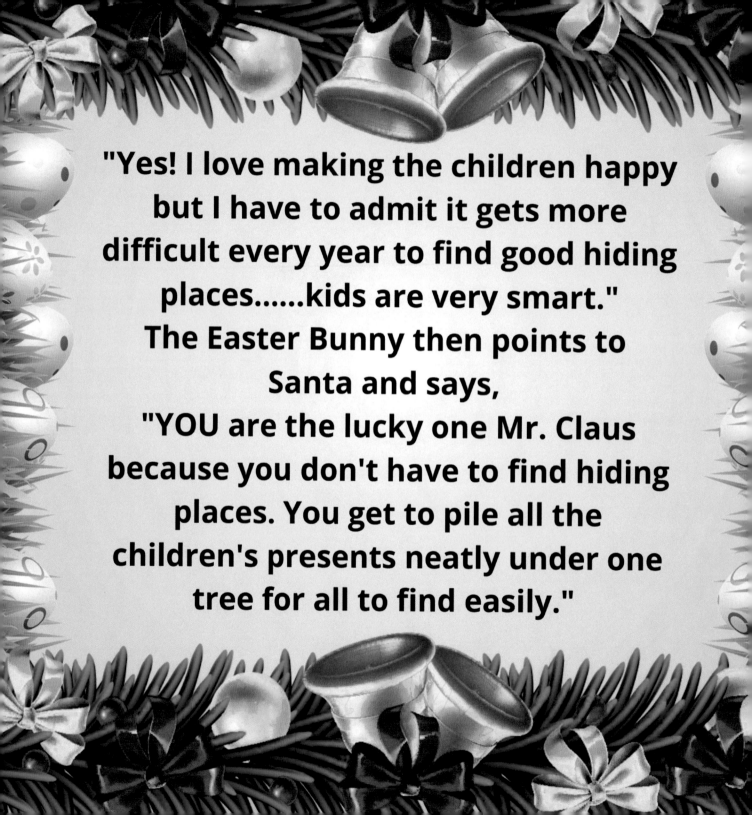

"Yes! I love making the children happy but I have to admit it gets more difficult every year to find good hiding places......kids are very smart."
The Easter Bunny then points to Santa and says,
"YOU are the lucky one Mr. Claus because you don't have to find hiding places. You get to pile all the children's presents neatly under one tree for all to find easily."

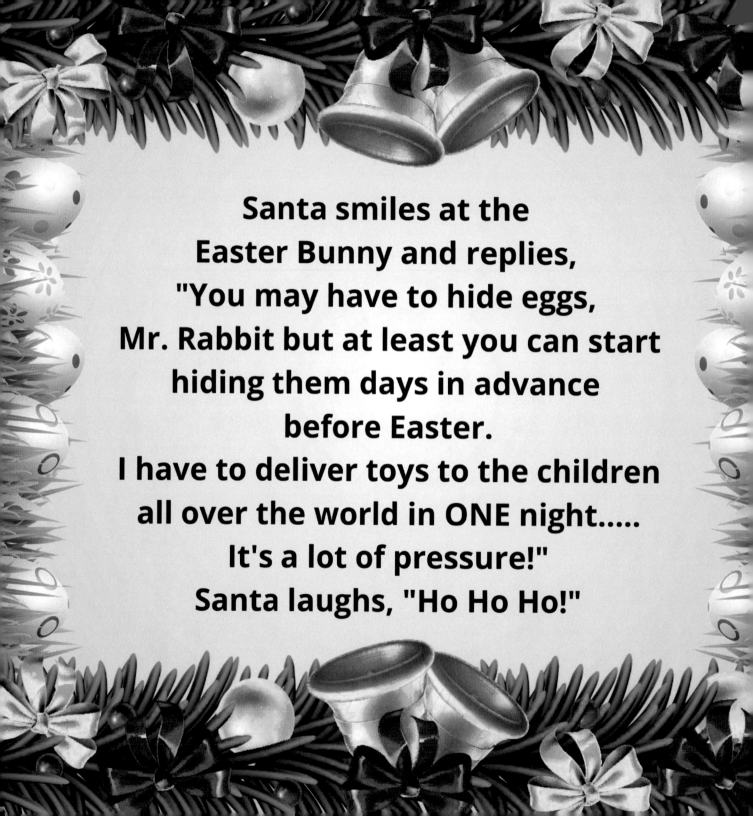

Santa smiles at the
Easter Bunny and replies,
"You may have to hide eggs,
Mr. Rabbit but at least you can start
hiding them days in advance
before Easter.
I have to deliver toys to the children
all over the world in ONE night.....
It's a lot of pressure!"
Santa laughs, "Ho Ho Ho!"

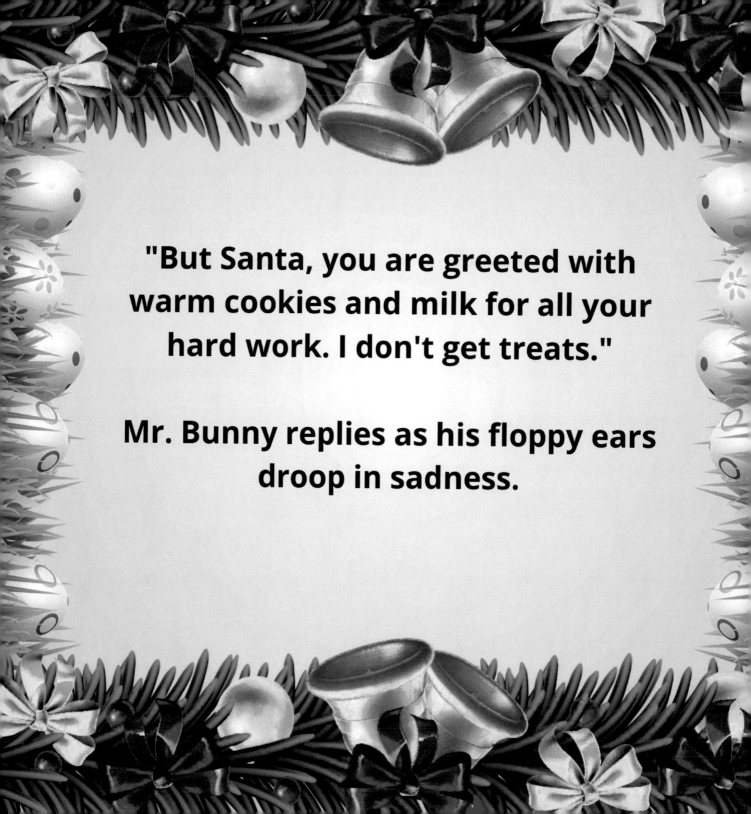

"But Santa, you are greeted with warm cookies and milk for all your hard work. I don't get treats."

Mr. Bunny replies as his floppy ears droop in sadness.

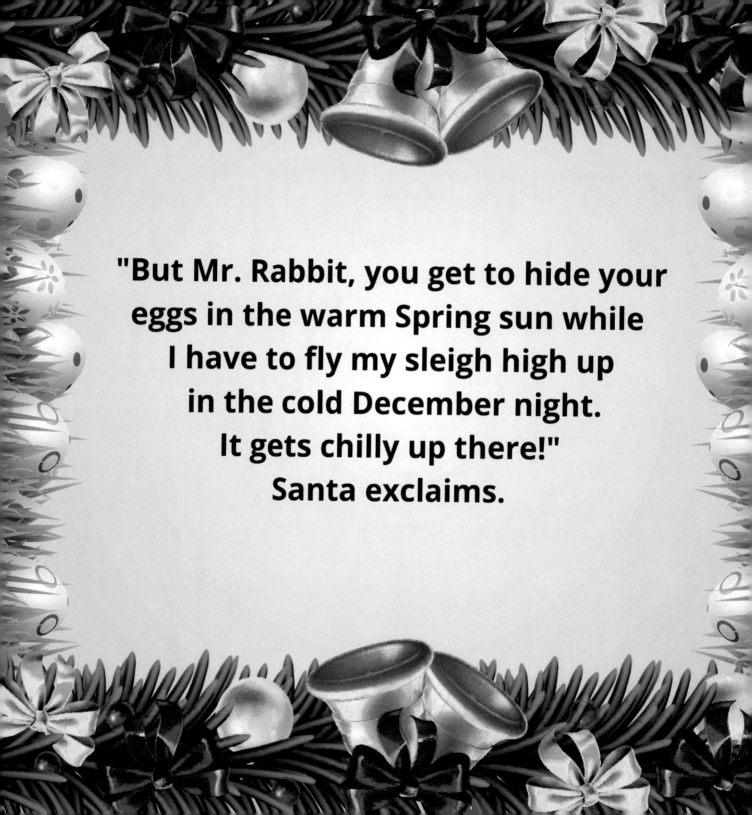

"But Mr. Rabbit, you get to hide your eggs in the warm Spring sun while I have to fly my sleigh high up in the cold December night. It gets chilly up there!" Santa exclaims.

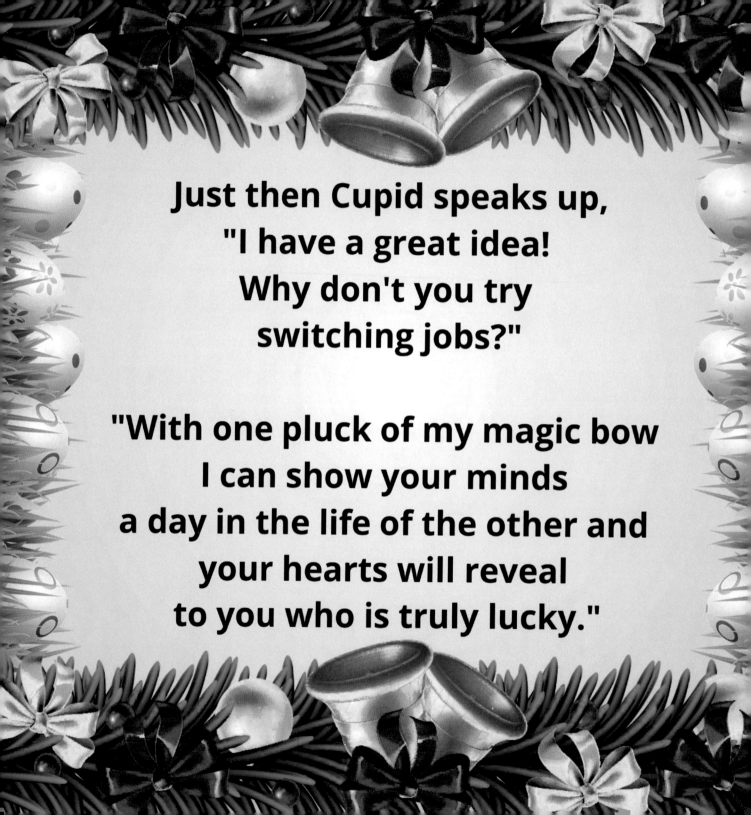

Just then Cupid speaks up,
"I have a great idea!
Why don't you try
switching jobs?"

"With one pluck of my magic bow
I can show your minds
a day in the life of the other and
your hearts will reveal
to you who is truly lucky."

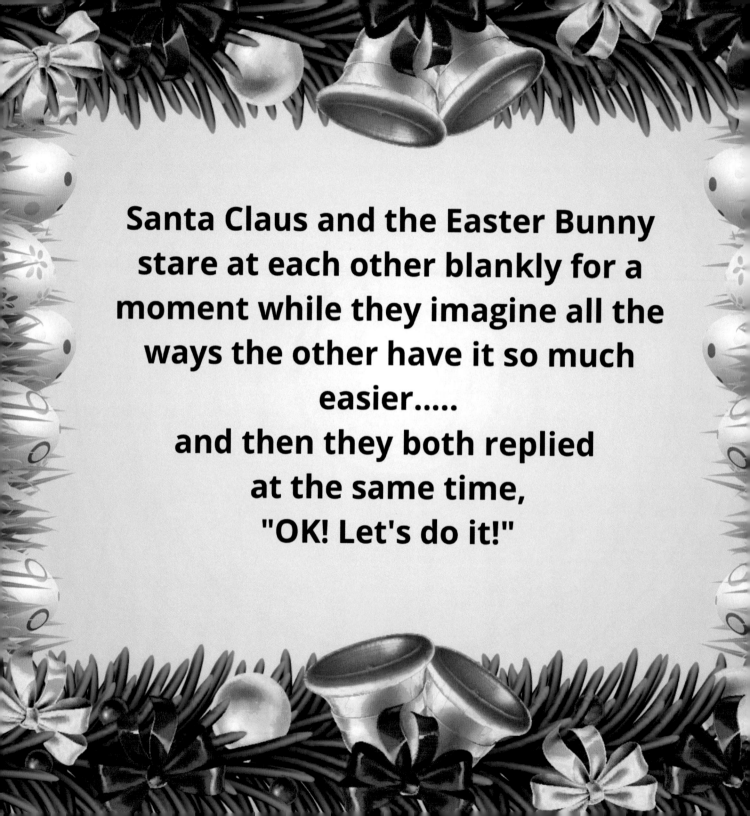

Santa Claus and the Easter Bunny stare at each other blankly for a moment while they imagine all the ways the other have it so much easier.....
and then they both replied at the same time,
"OK! Let's do it!"

The Easter Bunny felt a gentle tap from Cupid's bow then suddenly found himself flying high in the sky in Santa's sleigh.

"Wow! It really IS chilly up here!" The Easter bunny exclaims through chattering teeth.
"My thick bunny fur isn't enough to keep me warm in this cold December night...
I miss hopping around in the warm Spring air!"

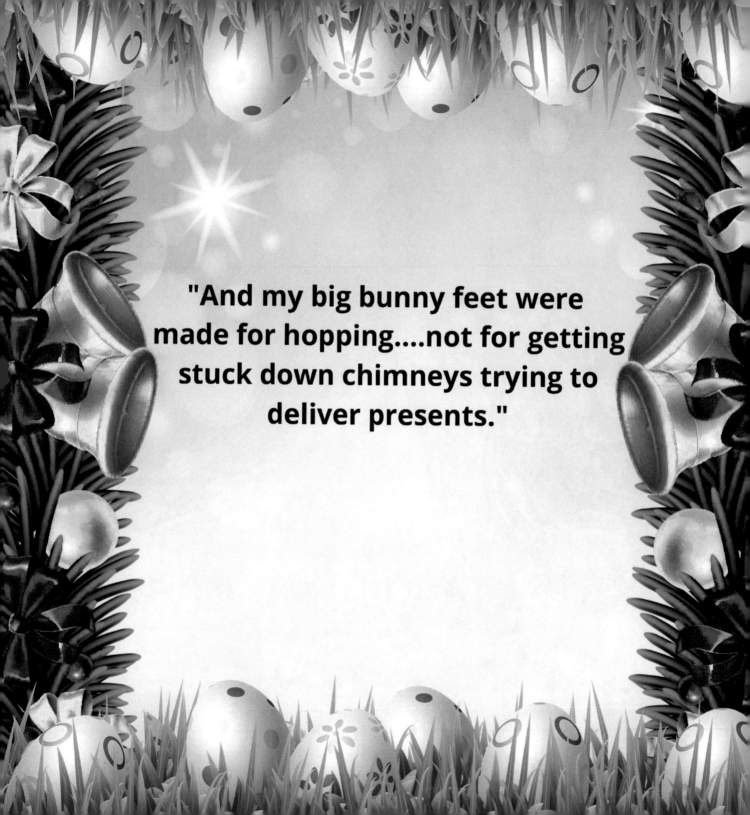

"And my big bunny feet were made for hopping....not for getting stuck down chimneys trying to deliver presents."

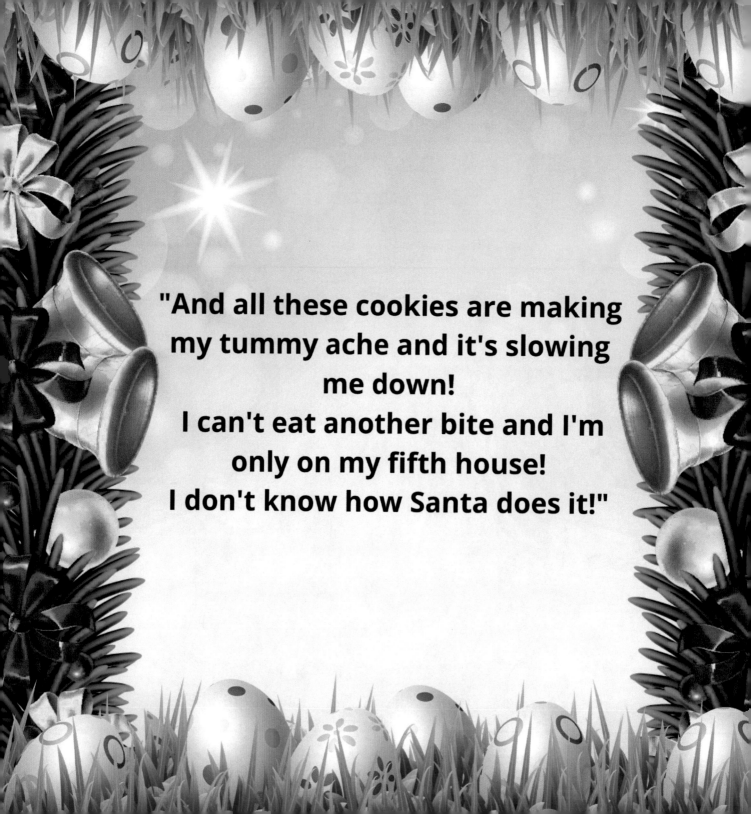

"And all these cookies are making my tummy ache and it's slowing me down!
I can't eat another bite and I'm only on my fifth house!
I don't know how Santa does it!"

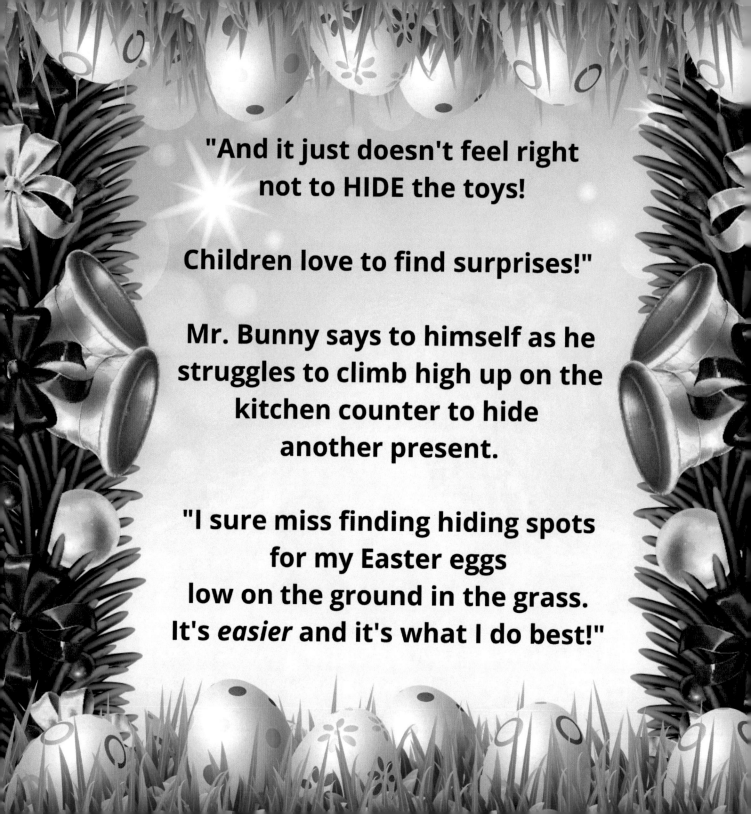

"And it just doesn't feel right
not to HIDE the toys!

Children love to find surprises!"

Mr. Bunny says to himself as he
struggles to climb high up on the
kitchen counter to hide
another present.

"I sure miss finding hiding spots
for my Easter eggs
low on the ground in the grass.
It's *easier* and it's what I do best!"

"It looks like the Easter Bunny has had quite an adventure delivering Christmas presents......

Now let's watch Santa as he lives a day in the life of hiding Easter eggs....."
Cupid giggles.

Santa suddenly finds himself in the warm Spring air loaded down with Easter eggs after feeling the tap of Cupid's bow.

"This weather is too hot for my thick winter coat and heavy boots.
I've been walking for hours trying to find hiding spots for these eggs.
I don't have big rabbit feet to help me hop fast......
I miss my fast sleigh and reindeer."
Santa grumbles as he trudges forward in the tall grass.

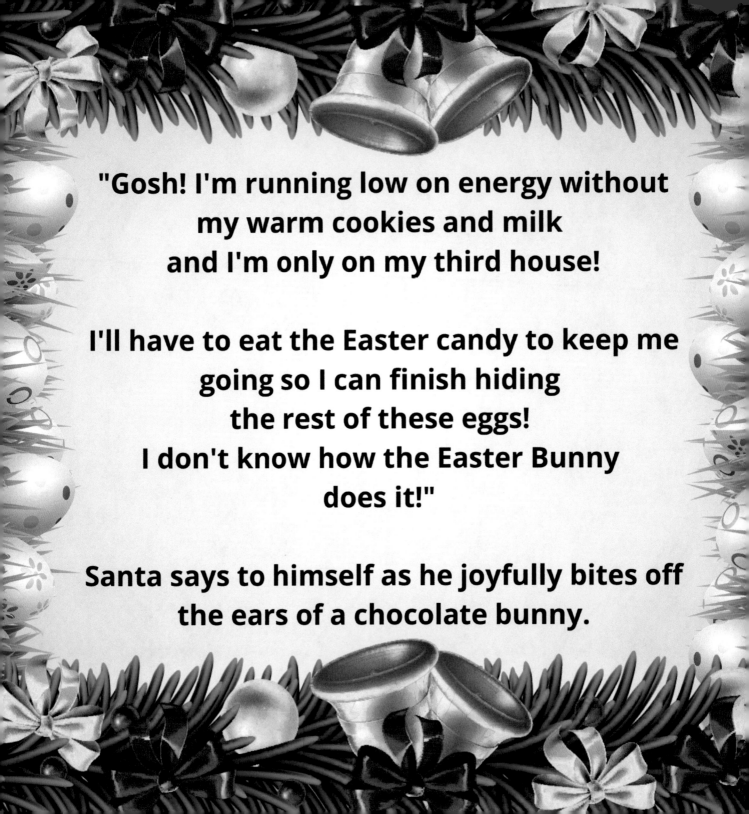

"Gosh! I'm running low on energy without
my warm cookies and milk
and I'm only on my third house!

I'll have to eat the Easter candy to keep me
going so I can finish hiding
the rest of these eggs!
I don't know how the Easter Bunny
does it!"

Santa says to himself as he joyfully bites off
the ears of a chocolate bunny.

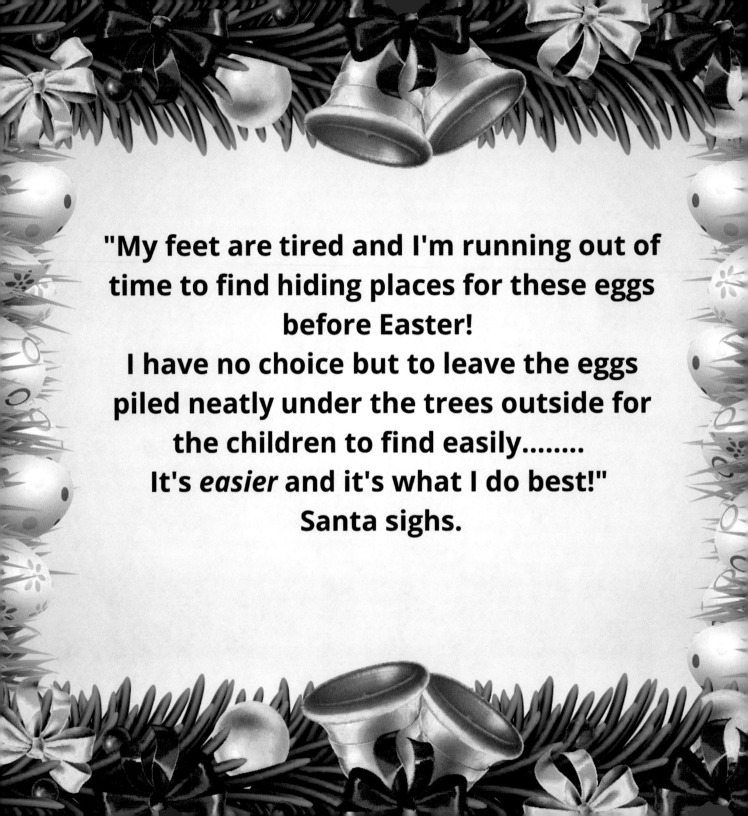

"My feet are tired and I'm running out of time to find hiding places for these eggs before Easter!
I have no choice but to leave the eggs piled neatly under the trees outside for the children to find easily........
It's *easier* and it's what I do best!"
Santa sighs.

"It looks like you two had quite an adventure.
Now lets watch the magic television to see how your actions effected the children all over the world."
Cupid says as he turns the channel to watch
the news on Christmas day.

The Easter Bunny and Santa watch in anticipation.....

"There is a global outcry this morning that Christmas has been ruined because there are no presents under the trees.

Reports continue to flood in that presents are being found in the strangest places.

One young girl found her new dolly in a cupboard with the pots and pans and is in tears because Santa didn't eat the cookies she left out for him.

Everyone is left in confusion today as we all wonder if Santa Claus no longer enjoys spreading joy to the children around the world." Reports the newscaster.

Cupid then turns the channel to watch the news report on Easter.....

"This just in......All the children's chocolate Easter bunny ears are mysteriously missing and there are no Easter egg hunts anywhere in the world.

All the eggs were found sitting neatly piled under a single tree in the front yard.....alongside several crumpled up candy wrappers.

Evidence strongly suggests that the Easter Bunny himself ate all the candy.
We are all baffled today as to why the Easter Bunny would be OK with making the children sad."
The newscaster reports.

Santa Claus and the Easter Bunny are both shocked at the upset they have caused the children around the world.

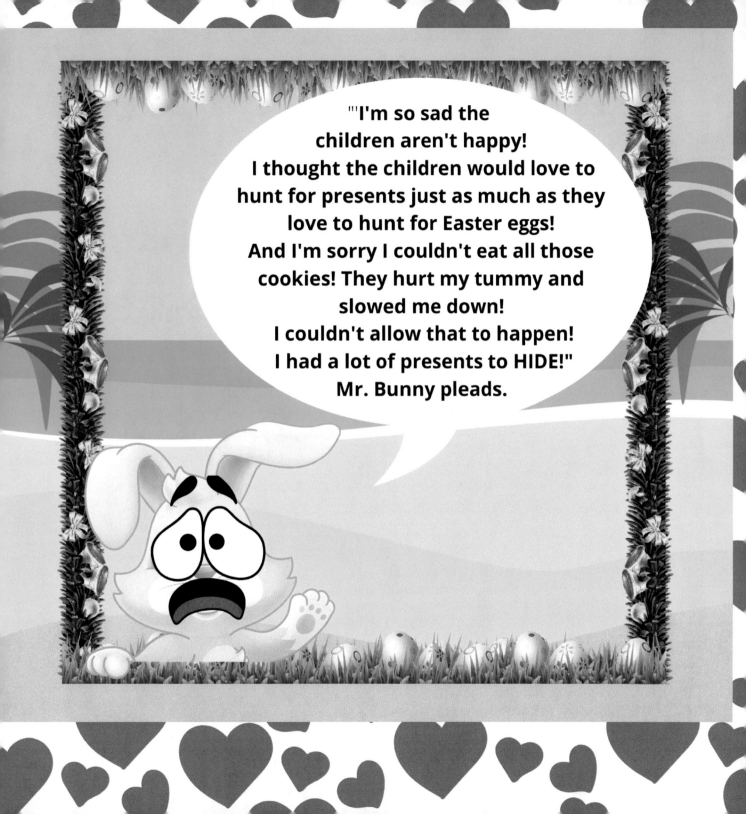

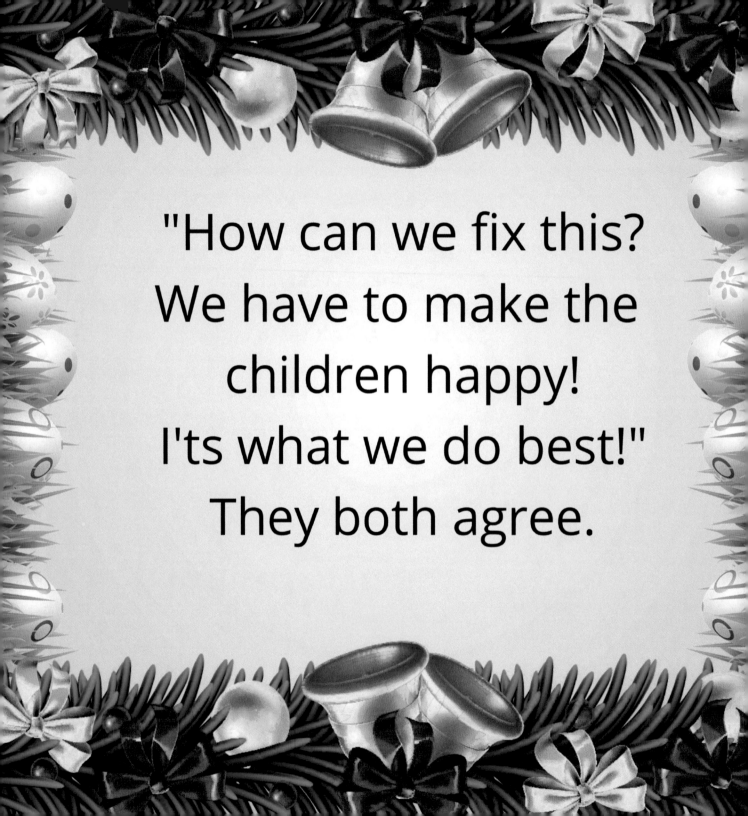

"How can we fix this?
We have to make the
children happy!
I'ts what we do best!"
They both agree.

"Don't worry!
I can easily fix this with just a few
more plucks of my magic bow!"
Cupid reassures his friends.
"I will return your minds back to
your own life....but only if you both
promise you have
learned your lesson."

"Do you still believe the other
has it easier?"
Cupid asks.

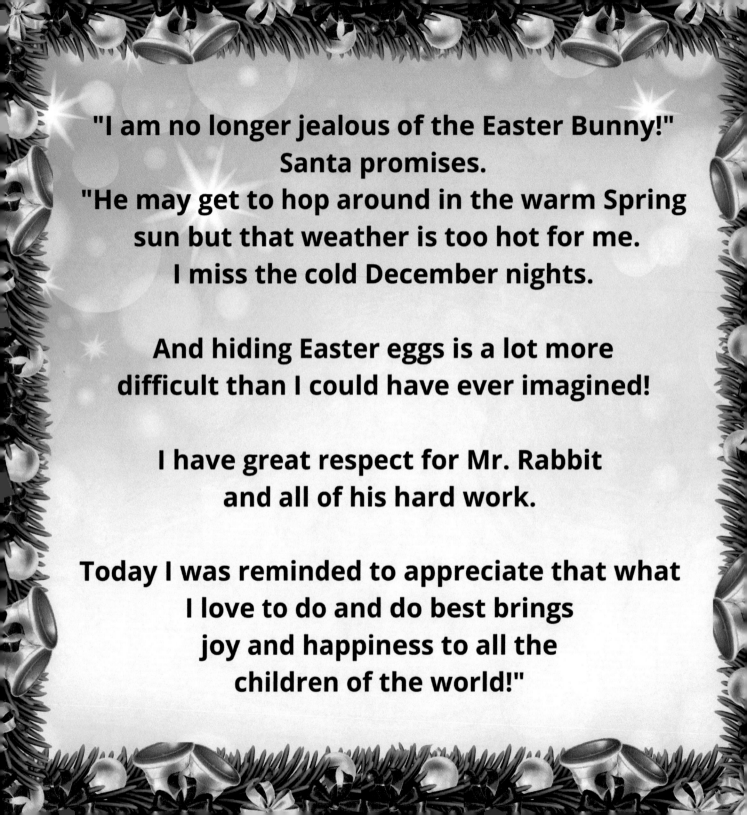

"I am no longer jealous of the Easter Bunny!"
Santa promises.
"He may get to hop around in the warm Spring
sun but that weather is too hot for me.
I miss the cold December nights.

And hiding Easter eggs is a lot more
difficult than I could have ever imagined!

I have great respect for Mr. Rabbit
and all of his hard work.

Today I was reminded to appreciate that what
I love to do and do best brings
joy and happiness to all the
children of the world!"

Suddenly Santa feels the quick tap of Cupid's bow!

."I am no longer jealous of Santa!"
Mr. Bunny says confidently.
"Flying high in Santa's sleigh in the
cold is not for me.
Delivering all those presents down chimneys
is a lot more difficult than I could
have ever imagined!
And he can have all those delicious cookies!
Hopping around after eating makes
my tummy hurt!
I have great respect for Santa and all
of his hard work.
Today I was reminded that what I love to do
and do best makes the children of the
world happy!"

Suddenly Love fills their hearts.
Santa Claus and
the Easter Bunny jump for joy
and cheer out,

*"We are BOTH unique
and special!"*

Cupid perks up and adds,
"And don't forget that we are

ALL UNIQUE

with our very own special
gifts and talents to share
with the world!

Especially

YOU!

Reading
THIS BOOK!"

 The End

"I'll see all of you on our next
vacation....and adventure!"
Cupid says with a wink and a smile.

Thank you for reading!
Reviews are kindly welcomed
on web site purchased!
Available at:
Amazon.com
BarnesandNoble.com

Made in the USA
Middletown, DE
06 November 2022

14179482R00031